The Art of the

WHITE

SHIRT

The Art of the

WHITE

SHIRT

Over 30 ways to
wear a white T-shirt,
blouse or shirt

Illustrated by

LIBBY VANDERPLOEG

hardie grant books

CONTENTS

INTRODUCTION

The white shirt is a perennial style classic.
Whether serving as a simple blank canvas or
dramatic structured centrepiece, it can be used
to enhance any outfit or occasion.

This book suggests looks for specific kinds of shirt,
but most can be adapted for any shirt you happen
to have in your wardrobe. Dotted throughout are
inspirational style icons who have each championed
the style staple in their own special way.

Master the art of the white shirt!

THE WHITE SHIRT IN STYLE

Let's unbutton the white shirt.

Like many of our most iconic womenswear garments, the white shirt evolved from menswear. We can trace it back to the Middle Ages when a simple collarless version was worn as a rough, nipple-chafing undergarment, through to the 1700s when Mr Darcy-style billowing linen blousons or frou-frou lace-edged versions were all the rage. By the late 1800s, when factory-made clothing became more accessible, a tailor-made shirt was a sure-fire symbol of men's prosperity and status. This was when Western women first started wearing the white shirt, and its slow liberation into womenswear began – edged on further by the temporary reversal of gender roles during World Wars I and II.

It's perhaps this menswear ancestry that makes the women's shirt something of a sexy construct; that rumpled, borrowed-from-the-boyfriend look that graces the cover of men's mags. But seeing the white shirt solely in terms of its relationship with men feels a little dated (and certainly wouldn't pass the Bechdel test). In a wonderfully modern way, the white shirt is genderless, a blank slate onto which designers and dressers can project their ideas.

In the same way denim jeans are an instant signifier of folksy authenticity, first worn by the blue-collar workers of early America, the white shirt feels instantly chic and utilitarian. It is easily as iconic as the quilted Chanel bag or the Burberry trench, but the white shirt is not tied down to a certain brand, or as potentially pretentious. The shirt is a constant source of interest to contemporary designers who can play up its smartness or loosen it up with an informal feel.

The white shirt looks best in a subtly relaxed fit, cut from rich white chambray, crumpled oxford, or crisp poplin (never 100 per cent man-made fibre), with pale buttons (perhaps mother of pearl) and simple tonal stitching. It doesn't need to be made by a luxury brand or hand-tailored on Savile Row, because in its simplest form, the white shirt is wonderfully sophisticated, considered and confident – and who doesn't want that?

Polished Popover

THEN ADD:

crisp cotton flat-front shorts

printed clutch

simple, elegant flats

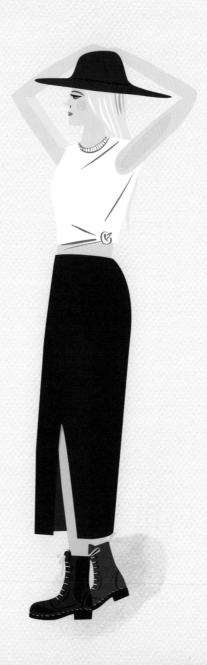

Comfy T

THEN ADD:

stretch-knit black tube skirt

broad-brimmed felt hat

distressed work boots

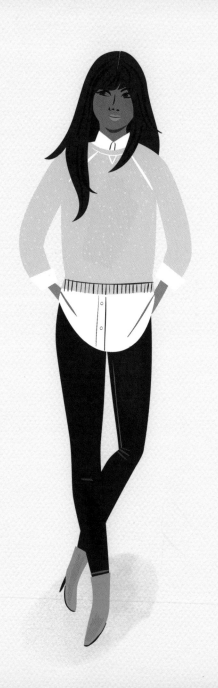

Crisp Button-Down

THEN ADD:

dark-rinse skinny jeans

knitted jumper

leather ankle boots

Style Icon

SOLANGE KNOWLES

It's not easy being the other Knowles, but Solange (born 1986) does it with style. As Beyoncé's sister, she may seem to be in the shadow of her whip-smart, super-talented sibling, but Solange is 100 per cent her own woman. The singer, song writer, sometime actor and artist has been releasing music since 2002, but it was the groundbreaking *True* (2012) created with Brit musician and producer Dev Hynes, that really developed – and underlined – Solange's unique sound and look.

> ## "Through style, you can communicate to the world who you are and what you stand for."
> — *Solange Knowles*

The white shirt has long been part of Solange's personal style, and she pulls her outfits together in a chic, contemporary way, often with a cloud of teased out, Afro-style hair. If her sister is all about raw glamour, big budget theatre, and short shorts, Solange has the sort of considered, indie look you'd see at a hipster flea market or dancing in the crowd at Afropunk rather than hair-flicking on stage at the Superbowl half-time show. It's a style that feels deeply personal and does its job in marking out Solange as a unique artist – less commercial and more idiosyncratic, perhaps. Little wonder that, at her wedding to Alan Ferguson in 2014, she styled all the guests in white and choreographed a performance with her son, and in the video for 'Losing You', Solange dances with the iconic Congolese fashion-obsessed dandies known as Les Sapeurs. With every song, album, and white shirt appearance, Solange assures us of her independence from the Knowles family. In the track 'God-Given Name' she sings, 'I'm not her and never will be.' Solange has spoken and it seems we're listening: in 2016 her third major release, *A Seat at the Table*, became her first number one album.

Oversized Button-Down

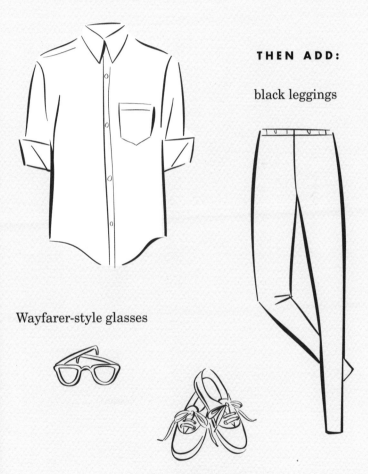

THEN ADD:

black leggings

Wayfarer-style glasses

black cotton tennis shoes

Backwards Collarless Blouse

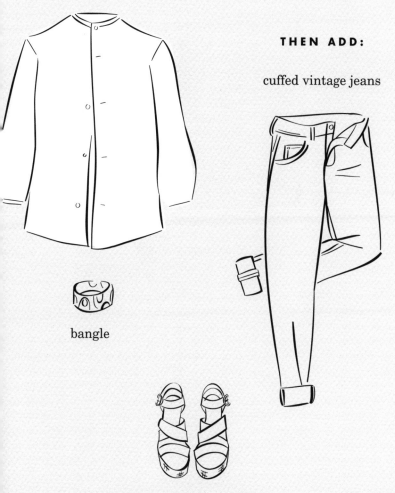

THEN ADD:

cuffed vintage jeans

bangle

strappy platform sandals

Short-Sleeved Shirt

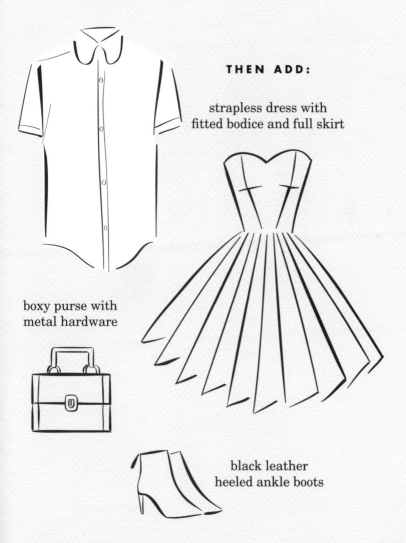

THEN ADD:

strapless dress with
fitted bodice and full skirt

boxy purse with
metal hardware

black leather
heeled ankle boots

Style Icon

KATHARINE HEPBURN

"Any time I hear a man say he prefers a woman in a skirt, I say, Try one. Try a skirt."

— Katharine Hepburn

A s a child, Katharine Hepburn (1907–2003) called herself Jimmy, cut her hair short, and became an avid swimmer, winning her first gold tournament at age 16. Her approach to gender wasn't just non-conformist, it did away with it altogether, and this F.U. attitude lent itself to her personal style. When charting the unique career of this celebrated Hollywood actor, her infamous white shirt and trousers are a good place to start.

In the 1930s, a woman in mannish get-up was lip-bitingly provocative, but Hepburn and a number of other actors (Greta Garbo, Marlene Dietrich) somehow wrestled trousers from the men – and survived. Hepburn was constantly thought of as too masculine, too aggressive: she scored her first film role in *A Bill of Divorcement* (1932), shortly after graduating from Bryn Mawr College, and – although the film was a hit – audiences bristled at her sharp, loud voice and confident physicality. But she blazed her way through a sexist Hollywood industry, and eventually commanded her own career.

She won an Oscar for *Morning Glory* (1933), and – after buying herself out of her contract with RKO – she starred in *The Philadelphia Story* (1950), first acquiring the rights, then selling them to MGM. She then spent 25 years making nine films with Spencer Tracy, (keeping their off-screen affair secret) and became an unforgettable star. Hepburn's enduring appeal is that she simply did things her own way. She was powerful, confident, and in her man trousers and white shirt she rolled up her sleeves and got things done.

Tied Button-Down

THEN ADD:

breezy culottes

chunky leather wedges

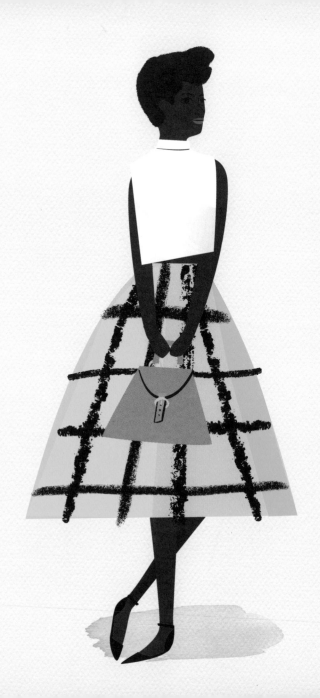

Cropped Mock Turtleneck

THEN ADD:

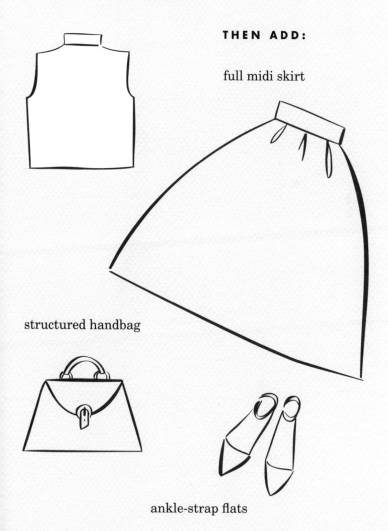

full midi skirt

structured handbag

ankle-strap flats

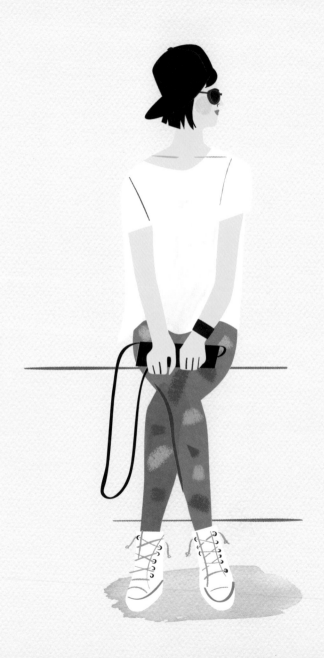

Open-Neck T

THEN ADD:

printed leggings

leather baseball cap

cross-body vagabond

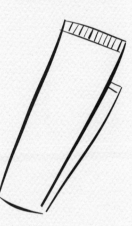

canvas high-tops

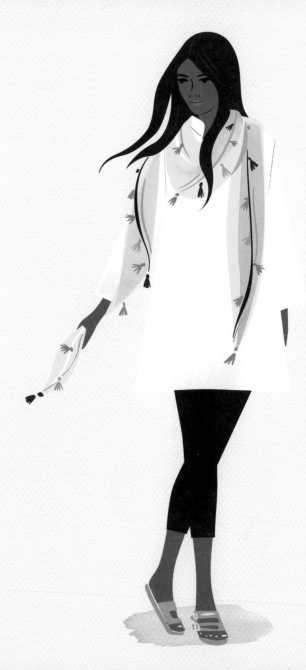

Linen Tunic

capri leggings

cork-soled sandals

soft pashmina

Style Icon

LEANDRA MEDINE

Leandra Medine (born 1988), the bangle-loving founder of wonderfully snark-free style site Man Repeller, carved out a career path from part-time blogger to major fashion influencer and Chief Creative Director with hefty ad income and a staff of editorial hotshots. She's a digital native with a rare quality: she's nice. Celebrating fashion (the Man Repeller MO is that women dress because they love style, not to impress men), feminism, and culture, MR goes further than most in analysing trends and unpacking their meanings.

> "I think what's so interesting for people is that I don't take it so seriously."
> — *Leandra Medine*

For Medine, the white shirt is a mainstay: it's what she's photographed in most, its simplicity underlined by the New Yorker's penchant for adding contrasting (and slightly crazy) pieces to her look, plus standout handbags and the odd 'arm party' – the gaggle of bracelets she likes to stack up her forearms. Medine's own style portraits are captioned with a solid mix of upbeat self-deprecation and humour, but there's an undeniably unique grasp of style in her output. In this way, she's leading by example, encouraging women to not care what others think – an approach that really found its audience in 2010 when Medine launched the site. As Medine and Man Repeller grow up, one thing that hasn't changed is her enthusiasm for fashion. Her outfits are as odd and oddly wearable as ever, and she continues to wear a white shirt, often tied in unusual ways, but the MR approach now goes a little deeper, answering the need for an intelligent, considered experience with matching accessories: style and substance, if you will.

Oversized Men's Shirt

THEN ADD:

slouchy cropped trousers

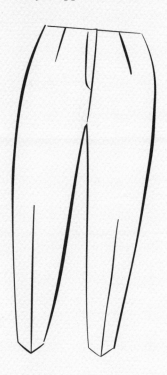

earrings
and bangles

metallic T-strap heels

Simple V-Neck T

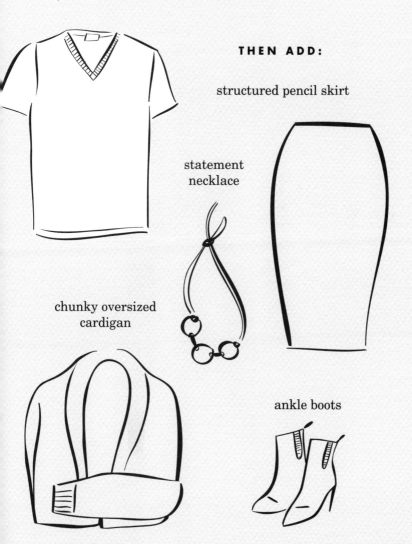

THEN ADD:

structured pencil skirt

statement
necklace

chunky oversized
cardigan

ankle boots

Gauzy Peasant Top

THEN ADD:

distressed boyfriend jeans

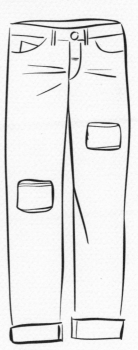

wooden-soled
sandals

simple leather tote

Style Icon

PATTI SMITH

At the age of 64, Patti Smith (1946) released the memoir *Just Kids*, a retreading of her mythical and magical youth with co-conspirator Robert Mapplethorpe in New York City. The pair were the perfect bohemians, making love and art, writing poetry, living for a time at the Chelsea Hotel, and scrambling around for cash so they could go celeb-spotting at Max's Kansas City as they moved ever closer to Warhol's inner circle. Smith ran with the creative gangs of New York, the debutantes and disco stars of the late 1970s to the early '80s heroes of the art and pop music scene who would dress up and show off at Max's, CBGBs and Studio 54.

> "No one expected me.
> Everything awaited me."
> — *Patti Smith*

Experimenting with her own style, Smith soon developed a look that became her life-long signature, and it was first captured by Mapplethorpe. He created the iconic image of her in a crumpled white shirt – from the Salvation Army store on Bowery – worn with black trousers and a black jacket slung over her shoulder. The photograph became the cover of *Horses*, her debut album, and is considered one of the most iconic album covers (and albums) of all time. There is something wonderfully louche and androgynous about the image; Smith had found her style and white shirts and mannish outfits have stayed a constant throughout her life. Now worn with beaten up boots, scuffed vintage denim jeans, blazers and dark frock coats, and a shaggy mop of dark grey hair, Smith is firmly at odds with most of her contemporaries (and most other septuagenarians) and all the cooler for it.

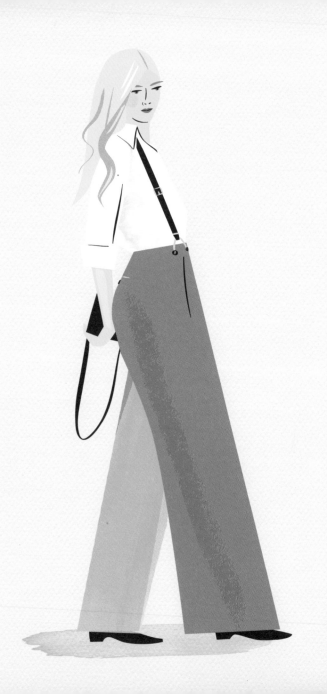

Slightly Fitted Oxford

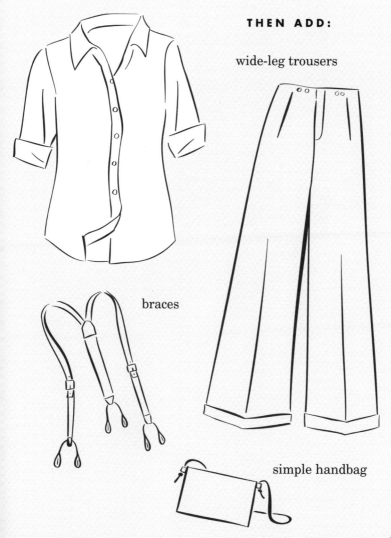

wide-leg trousers

braces

simple handbag

Sleek Sleeveless Blouse

tank pullover dress

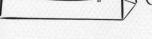

ross-body messenger bag

gladiator sandals

Wrap Shirt

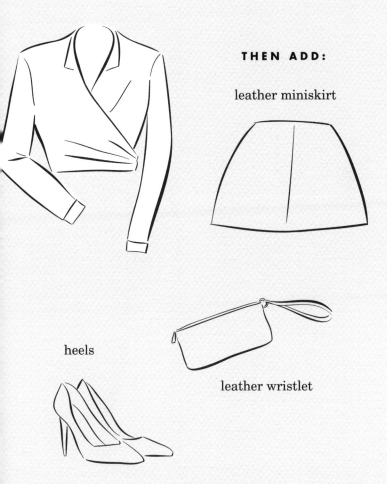

THEN ADD:

leather miniskirt

heels

leather wristlet

Style Icon

TILDA SWINTON

"I would rather be handsome for an hour than pretty for a week."

— *Tilda Swinton*

Is Tilda Swinton (born 1960) the world's coolest woman? The award-winning actor, producer, performance artist, and Scotland-based dog-lover is muse to countless film-makers (Wes Anderson, Luca Guadagnino, Bong Joon-ho), artists, and fashion designers. She juggles roles in big budget monster movies with celebrated art-house films, exclusive fashion events and grungy film festivals (once dragging a 33-tonne portable cinema screen across the Scottish Highlands), and frequently floors those who meet her with her charm, intelligence and otherworldliness.

Born in London, Swinton went to West Heath Girl's School with Princess Diana, the University of Cambridge (where she started performing on stage), and joined the Royal Shakespeare Company in 1984 before meeting and becoming the muse of Brit experimental film director Derek Jarman. On screen, she wears any number of fantastical creations, but off screen – and on the runway – she is at home in a simple white shirt.

Collaborating with Viktor & Rolf for their Fall/Winter 2003 collection, she infamously wore one on the runway, and has appeared in any number of androgynous cover shoots buttoned-up in white poplin for magazines like *Interview*, *i-D*, and *W*, with photographer Craig McDean reimagining her as David Bowie for *Vogue Italia*. As the face of a number of luxury brands, she also often slips into a white number for the red carpet, looking impossibly pulled together, leaving her contemporaries seeming a little trussed up. Easily done for the world's coolest woman.

Off-the-Shoulder Peasant Top

THEN ADD:

printed midi skirt

wedge espadrilles

Slim-Fitting Button-Down

THEN ADD:

wool sweater vest

winter shorts

ankle-strap heels

dark tights

mini leather backpack

Soft Victorian Blouse

high-waisted black jeans

bold-coloured heels

Style Icon

DIANE KEATON

A young Diane Keaton (born 1946) starred in a number of films throughout the 1970s – including Francis Ford Coppola's *The Godfather* – but it is the wonderfully wonky Woody Allen comedy *Annie Hall* that is considered to be Diane Keaton's real debut. *Annie* won Keaton her first Oscar in 1977 and to this day it's hard not to imagine the actor battling lobsters into a cooking pot. Keaton's Annie had an iconic, oddball look: billowing man trousers, natty waistcoat, kipper tie, battered wide brim hat and a rumpled white shirt. Keaton – who had a hand in Annie's costume design – borrowed from the cool-looking women of 1970s SoHo (the look has all the swagger of Patti Smith). Keaton and Allen's invention became an instant and enduring icon of style; still beloved today by fashion influencers and is endlessly referenced on the runway.

Although Keaton tried to distance herself from being cast as a 'kooky' actor after *Annie Hall*, she has borrowed from the character's style throughout her professional and personal career. White shirts and marvelously mannish suits have punctuated her performances – Keaton's look has seeped into other characters from *The Family Stone* to *The First Wives Club*, and IRL she makes her mark in a tux, a black bow tie, or a three-piece tweed suit.

As an actor, director of film (and two Belinda Carlisle videos, including 'Heaven is a Place on Earth'), real-estate developer, and image-maker (her curious photographic book of hotel lobbies has a cultish following), Keaton's own creativity stands out. Her white shirt continues to be a middle finger flip to the Hollywood establishment; she has never toed the line.

"Just have fun. Smile.
And keep putting on lipstick."
— Diane Keaton

Lightweight Shirt Dress

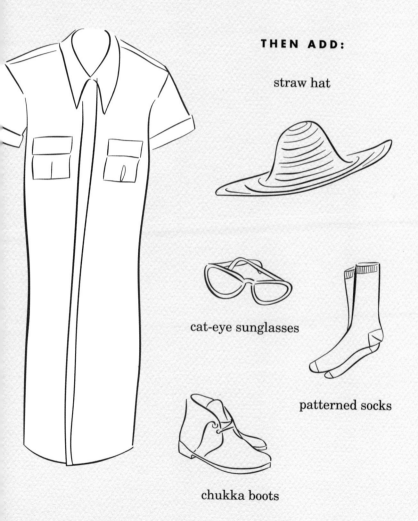

THEN ADD:

straw hat

cat-eye sunglasses

patterned socks

chukka boots

Oversized Shirt

cotton-knit racerback dress

printed headscarf

slip-on sneakers

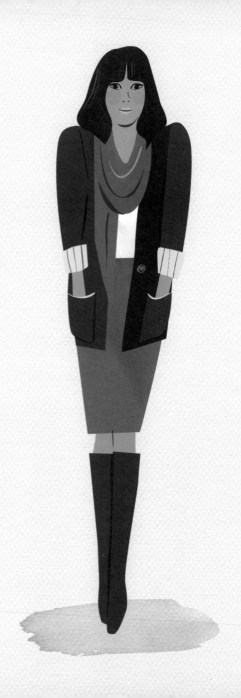

Basic T

THEN ADD:

blazer

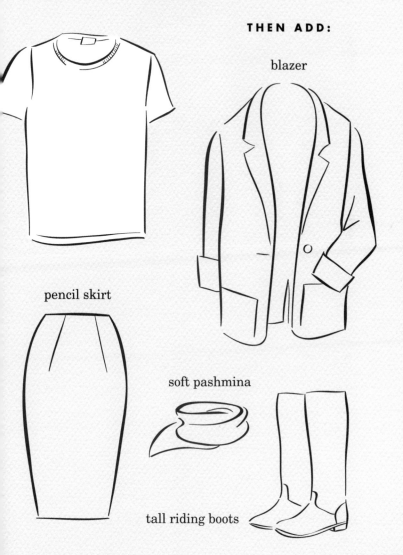

pencil skirt

soft pashmina

tall riding boots

Style Icon

ISABELLA ROSSELLINI

A nimal sex expert, activist, author, model, cult film actor, and daughter of cinematic royalty Ingrid Bergman and director Roberto Rossellini, Italian-American Isabella Rossellini (born 1954) moved from Rome to New York when she was 19. She went to college, acted as a translator and an Italian TV reporter, and became part of the NYC cool crew. She squeezed in a quick four-year marriage to Martin Scorcese (1979–1982), before appearing in films like David Lynch's *Blue Velvet* (1986) and *Death Becomes Her* (1992). With a somewhat capricious take on career goals, Rossellini is now an author and activist with an interest in animal behaviour, and her short film strand *Green Porno* is a celebrated lo-fi take on the sex antics of wildlife kingdom.

"True elegance is for me the manifestation of an independent mind."
— Isabella Rossellini

In a life lived by her own rules, Rossellini has always done things her own way, not least in an approach to style that has long played with gender norms. Her short, boyish hair and love of the white shirt are part of this. At the age of 28, Bruce Weber shot her for British *Vogue* and her modelling career began (late in life by today's standards). Other shoots followed, and Rossellini found herself collaborating on imagery by Richard Avedon, Helmut Newton, Steven Meisel, even Robert Mapplethorpe. Each photographer helped hone Rossellini's style, and the white shirt became a more integral part of her everyday outfit – a boyish, powerful look she wears to this day.

Backwards Oversized Button-Down

THEN ADD:

flared jeans

cotton canvas sneakers

Slouchy T

THEN ADD:

camel hair coat

denim shirt

oxfords

cuffed skinny jeans

Style Icon

DIANA, PRINCESS OF WALES

I n 2013, Grammy-award-winning 'S&M' singer Rihanna revealed something rather unexpected: she had a style icon few would have thought had been so influential to her look. Diana, Princess of Wales, was her sometime fashion inspiration, reminding us of the enduring significance, intrigue and fever-pitch fascination with the late, great royal.

Diana Spencer (1961–1997), the young, shy, and famously doe-eyed British noble, became an object of obsession for the international tabloid press following her marriage to Charles, Prince of Wales, in 1981, which was watched by 750 million people. Suddenly navigating fandom previously unknown in the pre-social-media age, Diana became a style icon right up until her death in 1997.

"I don't go by the rulebook... I lead from the heart, not the head."
— Diana, Princess of Wales

Away from the ballgowns and event wear, her off-duty look was a mash-up of preppy essentials, stonewash jeans, and sporty tops, and her go-to piece was the white shirt. She would wear it with luxe knits and chinos, adding a black skinny bow or frilly pie-crust collar. Loved by the Sloane Rangers – the Diana-wannabes associated with the exclusive Sloane Square neighbourhood in London – the white shirt soon became stuck in the collective fashion consciousness. In the 1980s, Diana fans accessorised it with a simple string of pearls, blue eyeliner, or perhaps a velvet padded hair band, but contemporary times are less straight-laced. Rihanna adds skinny jeans, a leather skirt, or a whole lotta thigh: perhaps not quite how Diana would have worn it, but fit for a princess, all the same.

Broken-In Button-Down

THEN ADD:

cuffed denim overalls

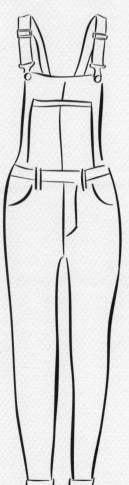

ankle boots

chunky glasses

Tunic Blouse

black leggings

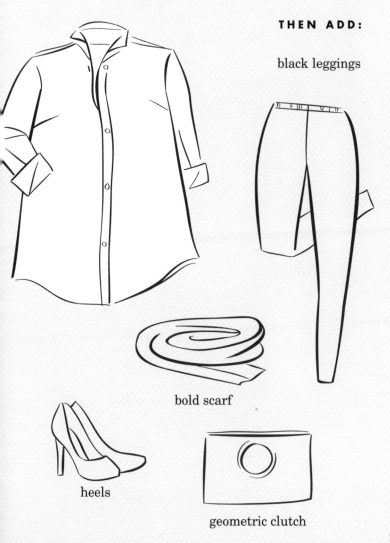

bold scarf

heels

geometric clutch

Style Icon

CAROLINA HERRERA

"Just wear what you think looks beautiful."

— Carolina Herrera

Venezuelan-American designer Carolina Herrera (born 1939) is in no doubt over the power of the white shirt. In a career that spans more than three decades, the white shirt has been integral to Herrera's collections; a vital aspect of her classy (yet never pretentious) signature style. First Ladies, from Jackie O to Michelle Obama, along with an army of celebs from Olivia Palermo to Karlie Kloss, seem to agree.

Herrera first presented a white shirt in her debut collection in 1981 and it's been a garment she returns to ever since. She makes much of its versatility, believing its goes-with-anything quality is the reason it has cropped up in women's wardrobes again and again. In this way, there's something mildly reactionary to the white shirt: it's a lip-curl to current trends, a shunning of fast fashion, and membership to an exclusive club of women who are confident about their own personal style.

In the 60s, a well-connected Herrara worked for Emilio Pucci in Caracas, became a regular on International Best Dressed lists, and moved to New York in 1980, falling in with the Warhol set at Studio 54. As a child, her grandmother had taken her to fashion shows, dressing her in upscale European brands, and helped hone her eye for style. Another grandmotherly figure, her friend Diana Vreeland, Editor-in-Chief of *Vogue*, suggested Herrera try her hand at design, and she did just that. Success came quickly, and the Carolina Herrera brand was born. It's hard to say if Herrera's success was built on the simple white shirt, but Herrera's clever understanding of the codes of fashion – and power of versatile, timeless pieces – is definitely something to do with it.

Cropped Boxy Blouse

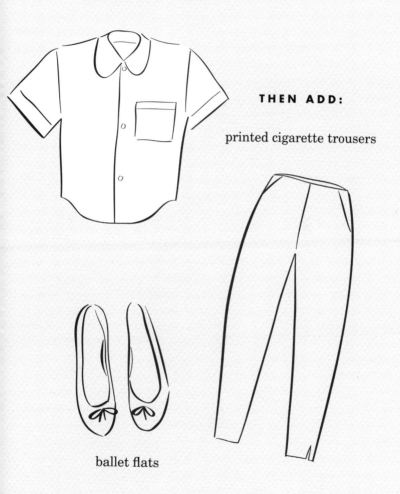

THEN ADD:

printed cigarette trousers

ballet flats

Square-Neck Top

THEN ADD:

rope necklace

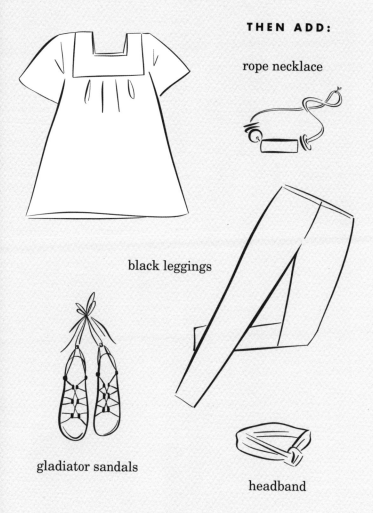

black leggings

gladiator sandals

headband

Scoop-Neck T

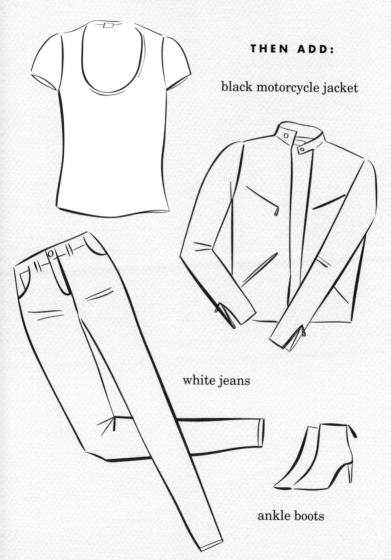

THEN ADD:

black motorcycle jacket

white jeans

ankle boots

Style Icon

JANELLE MONÁE

Fembots are taking over the world – and pop music is their first target. Janelle Monáe (born 1985) is the tuxedo-wearing Grammy-award-nominated recording artist, actor, and self-confessed android. The sci-fi obsessed star – who suggests she's of the robotic variety in her more infamous profile pieces – is known for her genre-mashing music, unique art direction, and doing it her own way.

Navigating the music industry can be a tricky affair. With major labels controlling their image, artists are restyled, and women often find themselves squished into short shorts and side-boob outfits rather than being able to rely on the strength of their talent. Here, Monáe is more than a few steps ahead. She is signed to her own imprint, Wondaland Arts Society, makes her own creative decisions, and is the master of her own look: tux-inspired outfits, crisp white shirts, and breathtakingly high hairdos. In a way, her monochrome look and saddle oxfords hark back to the 18th century, but Monáe adds a futuristic edge. She transcends trends as well as what is expected of her as a female recording artist.

"Embrace what makes you unique, even if it makes others uncomfortable."
— *Janelle Monáe*

Monáe sees the tux as a genderless outfit, and her geeky love affair with sci-fi is a clever entry point to explore otherness: race, sexuality, and gender. It's an approach that resounds with other musicians, and Monáe has scored collaborations with Prince, Erykah Badu, Solange Knowles, Nile Rogers, Duran Duran, and Grimes. Landing a role in the movie *Hidden Figures* (2017) was another unexpected step: she plays one of an almost-forgotten group of black female NASA mathematicians in 1969 – a perfectly fitting tale for the sci-fi style icon.

Sharp Shirt

THEN ADD:

full black skirt

sequined clutch

glittery heels

Cropped T

THEN ADD:

dungaree dress

retro sunglasses

canvas high-tops

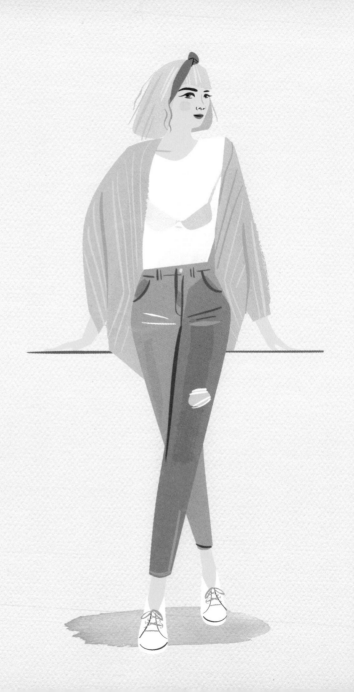

Loose Sheer T

black bra

distressed jeans

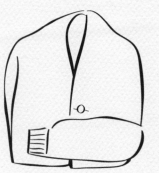

grandpa sweater

headscarf

canvas sneakers

HOW TO CARE FOR YOUR WHITE SHIRT

Perhaps you're stealth-eating a burger in the back of an Uber, or one-handedly Instagram scrolling while drinking a Pumpkin Spice latte, and tragedy befalls you. You'll find your favourite white shirt is a magnet to avocado smears, spaghetti sauce dribbles, and matcha tea splatters. Move quickly: don't let a stain dry; instead deal with it immediately. Be prepared to dab with baby wipes if you're away from home, but if you're in the privacy of your own lair, take off your shirt and spray with stain remover. After an hour, soak in a high quality laundry stain detergent. Follow by gently sponging the offending area if it's a bad one. Oh, and a word on those unsightly armpit marks: they're usually caused by aluminium-based anti-perspirants which stain and start to destroy fabric. Use a gentle deodorant instead.

On its first wash, your white shirt might shrink a little – but only by a smidge. Wash it separately to your dark clothes and use a cool temperature (a high setting will make the fabric brittle, dry and eventually it could rip), and follow the care instructions which, apparently, are there for a reason. Use a good quality detergent (avoid biological where possible) and hang it as soon as possible after washing; most of the creases will fall out as it dries. For best results, iron when it's still slightly damp with the steam setting on high – you want it hot and sultry. Dry-cleaning can leave a smart, crisp finish but does start to wear down the structure of the fabric, shortening its lifespan. Treat your white shirt with respect and it will serve you well.

THE ART OF THE WHITE SHIRT

First published in 2017 by Hardie Grant Books

Hardie Grant Books (UK)
52–54 Southwark Street
London SE1 1UN
hardiegrant.co.uk

Hardie Grant Books (Australia)
Ground Floor, Building 1
658 Church Street
Melbourne, VIC 3121
hardiegrant.com.au

British Library Cataloguing-in-Publication Data. A catalogue record
for this book is available from the British Library.

ISBN: 978-1-78488-087-3

Publisher: Kate Pollard
Senior Editor: Kajal Mistry
Editorial Assistant: Hannah Roberts
Publishing Assistant: Eila Purvis
Illustrator: Libby VanderPloeg
Art Direction: Libby VanderPloeg
Colour Reproduction by p2d

Printed and bound in China by 1010

10 9 8 7 6 5 4 3 2 1